T0130064

YOUR PURPOSE KNOWN
✚REVEALS✚
YOUR WEALTH
AND PROSPERITY

Wealth Is Stored Up for the Righteous

Ecclesiastes *10:19 KJV*
*… money answers **all** things*

BERNITA BURRIES-MASON

authorHOUSE®

AuthorHouse™
1663 Liberty Drive
Bloomington, IN 47403
www.authorhouse.com
Phone: 1 (800) 839-8640

Published by AuthorHouse 02/25/2019

ISBN: 978-1-5462-7308-0 (sc)
ISBN: 978-1-5462-7306-6 (hc)
ISBN: 978-1-5462-7307-3 (e)

Library of Congress Control Number: 2018915045

Print information available on the last page.

CONTENTS

All Astrid's (*) are author assertions

ABOUT THIS BOOK

This easy to read, take anywhere pocket book will empower you with scriptures and will indeed reveal that God has created you with His purpose to prosper you on **earth**. This pocket book will help you see that wealth is stored up just for you. You must reach for your purpose with an understanding that God endowed us all with a natural purpose in life. The purpose which includes the core passions within you, dreams, gifted abilities and Holy Spirit revealed wisdom. Seek out yours and your children's purpose. *How do you do this?* Simply ask the Lord to reveal it to you and He will. Most times it is noticeable in childhood. Seek God for this wisdom from above. *"The earth is the LORD'S, and the fulness thereof; the world, and they that dwell therein" Psalms 24:1.*

This book will direct you; provide scripture verses to help you renew your thinking, walk in peace, become wealthy, how to invest and obtain prosperity by God's ways of doing things; and avoid getting sidetracked but stay in the secret place of the most-high God. It will equip you with scriptures to remind you how to keep His commandments once you are prospering in your God given wealthy purpose in life.

This book has a host of scriptures to back up the fact that everyone has a purpose in life, and God's word states *"I wish above all things that you prosper and be in health even as your soul prospers". 3 John 1:2*

INTRODUCTION

My soul (mind) had to be reconditioned to receive that wealth belonged to me

I grew up in the church as a child. I would always hear the phrase "money is the root to all evil" from people in my daily surroundings in and out of the church. Therefore, growing up my thinking was framed to believe it was better to lack and "prosperity" was definitely a bad word in my world. I have a large family and witnessed firsthand financial struggles. I heard people confessing lack *all the time*, not understanding the power of the tongue (you have what you say). My mother was an awesome lady and a great provider. She did the best she could with very little money. I guess I can say that we were on the poor side and lacking finances. There was never enough money. However, the lack of finances was kept hidden from us children. We were always dressed well, and great values were imparted in the family.

To make my long story very short, as a child I always felt and knew within my heart and mind I was going to live in abundance as an adult. I began talking to God during my childhood. By the eighth grade (middle school), no one knew I had made a declaration to myself that wealth would transpire into my life at a particular age. I started to see God had endowed me with a purpose to live an abundant life in my late twenties/early thirties after discovering my purpose in life. I felt like a breakthrough in my soul took place. A light came on, then planning took root and never ceased. My mindset had to be *reborn* into a new dimension, which included God ways and plans of living a prosperous life.

Conclusion

I want to thank you for your precious time reading and using this pocket book. I trust you are even more inspired from biblical facts that God's word clearly reveals wealth and prosperity belong to you! Stay blessed.

+

CHAPTER 1

BE CONFIDENT ... YES... THE HEAVENLY FATHER GOD WANTS YOU TO PROSPER IN WEALTH ON EARTH!

1

This chapter will revitalize, enlighten and encourage you with scriptures that will empower you with self-assurance, wisdom and knowledge from God's word stating you are supposed to walk in wealth on earth. Enabling you to perceive the Lord as the ultimate source to revealing your purpose, wealth and prosperity. The Lord is the principal source to show you the way to get your wealth. It will simply change your mind-set.

1. BE CONFIDENT... YES... THE HEAVENLY FATHER GOD WANTS YOU TO PROSPER IN WEALTH ON EARTH!

Ecclesiastes 10:19 *KJV*
... ... but money answereth All things.

◊

Isaiah 48:17 *KJV*
Thus, says the LORD, your Redeemer, the Holy One of Israel: "I am the LORD your God, who teaches you to profit, who leads you in the way you should go.

(*God teaches and expects us to profit on earth. It is imperative for you to <u>find out your purpose on earth,</u> then act in it moving forward. This is when the Holy Spirit will start showing you secrets. The Holy Spirit is the Comforter, the third person of the trinity (Father, Son and Holy Spirit). Do you remember when Jesus said, I will send you a Comforter (helper)? (a) The way to connect with Him is by praying in the Spirit without ceasing. My experience is whenever I start praying in the Holy Spirit

5

my soul gets energized and the Lord truly does start communicating to me. He is so awesome! The Heavenly Father operates in the heavenly dimension "the secret place", this is where Jesus loves to meet with us. I call it my prayer closet. We have to worship Him in the spirit realm through Jesus Christ who is the only way to get the Father's attention. Talking to God is as simple as if you are having a conversation with your best friend. You start by having a personal relationship with the Lord, entering into His presence with thanksgiving, praise and worship. (b) This is the key).

Scripture References
(a) Matthew 14:26
(b) Psalms 100:4

◊

3 John 1:2 KJV
Beloved, <u>I wish above all things</u> that <u>thou</u> mayest <u>prosper</u> and be in health even as thy soul prospereth.

(*I simply take God at His word. I confess daily great health and wealth over my family and me. The bible is His word and it works. He said His word will not return

back to Him cancelled (a) and He cannot lie (b). <u>Without</u> <u>faith</u> it is impossible to please Him (c). When you talk with the Lord, by faith, allow your heart and mind to open, believe and trust His word. He truly will hear and answer your prayer, sometimes immediately. Do not doubt. He is waiting on you to ask, then He will answer.)

Scripture References
  (a) Isaiah 55:11
  (b) Numbers 23:19
  (c) Hebrews 11:6

◊

Jeremiah 1:5 KJV

Before <u>I formed</u> thee in the belly <u>I knew you</u>; and before thou camest forth out of the womb I sanctified thee, and I ordained thee a prophet unto the nations.

(*Wow, God knew all about me before I entered the earth. He dedicated, approved, designed and enabled me to do business and write by His grace and mercy, fulfilling my wealthy purpose on earth. This is why you have to find out your purpose from Him. This proves He is the source of our wealth)

◊

Proverbs 13:22 *KJV*

A good man leaveth an inheritance to his children's children: and the wealth of the sinner is laid up for the just.

(* *If you walk in your known purpose;* it will give you the ability to leave an inheritance for your grandchildren.)

◊

Psalm: 23 *KJV*

The LORD is my shepherd;
I shall not want...

(*I talked about my childhood financial experiences in the introduction of this book. When I learned the revelation of this verse which is God planned that

I will not live in poverty or lack for anything. This ignited the covenant and the confidence within my heart and *changed my thinking about money to God's way.*)

◊

Proverbs 18:21 KJV

Death and life are in the power of your tongue; and they that love it shall eat the fruit thereof.

(*God's word is full of directions to help us get the victory on earth. It frees us from all types of situations. The power of what you say in your circumstances will manifest your outcome. The true fact is you get what you say. Speak victory and not negative words when faced with situations. This stops negative forces.)

◊

Matthew 6:33 KJV

But seek ye first the kingdom of God, and his righteousness; and all these things shall be added unto you.

(*The Kingdom of God on earth concerns salvation, where you are in the Heavenly family relationship on earth. You first have to know Jesus Christ in order to have access to the Father, again salvation. Then you can seek His righteousness related to your purpose

and He will unveil secrets to you concerning yourself and your purpose.)

◊

Proverbs 23:7 KJV
For as he thinketh in his heart, so *is* he:

(*What you <u>think</u> in your heart about yourself is also how people see you, as you see yourself. This is just like the power of the tongue, you are thinking it instead of voicing it. Learn how to encourage yourself.)

◊

Ecclesiastes 5:19 KJV
Every man also to whom <u>God hath given riches</u> and wealth, <u>and</u> hath given him <u>power to eat thereof</u>, and to take his portion, and to rejoice in his labour; <u>this is</u> the <u>gift of God</u>.

(* Take heed to the underlined words.)

◊

Luke 12:7 *KJV*
But even the very hairs of your head are all numbered. <u>Fear not</u> therefore: <u>ye are of more value</u> than many sparrows.

(* Take heed to the underlined words)

◊

Psalm 37:25 *KJV*
I have been young, and now am old; yet have I <u>not seen</u> the <u>righteous forsaken, nor his seed begging bread</u>.

(* Take heed to the underlined words. God's plan is for you and your children to prosper)

◊

1 Timothy 6:17-19 *KJV*
[17]Charge them that are rich in this world, <u>that they be not highminded</u>, nor trust in uncertain riches, but in the living <u>God, who giveth us richly all things to enjoy</u>; [18]That they do good, that they be rich in good works, ready to distribute, willing to communicate; [19] <u>Laying up in store for themselves a good</u>

<u>foundation</u> against the time to come, that they may lay hold on eternal life.

(*Be confident the heavenly Father God wants you to prosper in wealth <u>on earth</u>.. Take heed to the underlined words.)

◊

Proverbs 21:20 *KJV*
²⁰ <u>There is treasure</u> to be desired and <u>oil in the dwelling of the wise</u>; but a foolish man spendeth it up.

◊

Philippians 4:19 *KJV*
But my <u>God</u> shall <u>supply</u> all your <u>need</u> according to his riches in glory in Christ Jesus.

(*Be confident the heavenly Father God wants you to prosper in wealth <u>on earth</u>.. Take heed to the underlined words.)

◊

2 Corinthians 9:8 *KJV*
And <u>God is able</u> to <u>make</u> all <u>grace abound toward you</u>; that ye, always having all

sufficiency in all things, may abound to every good work.

(*God's grace; the grace of God is powerful and highly critical to you being able to accept the fact the Lord <u>created you</u> qualified to walk in your purpose. Grace and purpose go together, especially for those who think they do not deserve to receive anything from the Lord. If you ask the Lord to reveal your purpose, He will. Get on one accord with Him knowing He loves you and has plans to fulfill your purpose on earth. Grace is a treasure from the Lord. Research the secrets about the grace of God concerning you. God has created us all different!)

◊

Proverbs 18:11 KJV
A <u>rich man's wealth</u> <u>is his strong city</u>, and like a high wall in his imagination.

(* Take heed to the underlined words)

◊

Ecclesiastes 10:19 *KJV*
A feast is made for laughter,
and wine maketh merry: but
money answereth all things.

*(*Be confident the heavenly Father God
wants you to prosper in wealth <u>on earth</u>.
Take heed to the underlined words.)*

◊

2 Corinthians 8:9 *KJV*
For you <u>know the grace</u> of our Lord Jesus
Christ, that, though He was rich, yet for
<u>your sake He</u> <u>became</u> poor, that ye through
<u>His</u> poverty might become rich.

*(*God sent His son, Jesus, to earth to show
us the way. We have been set free of poverty.
Jesus was chastised for your peace. Known
purpose leads to a peace of mind.)*

◊

Proverbs 8:18-21 *KJV*
[18]Riches and honour are with me; yea,
<u>durable riches and righteousness.</u> [19]My
fruit is better than gold, yea, than fine
gold; and my revenue than choice silver.

²⁰I lead in the way of righteousness, <u>in the midst of the paths</u> of judgment: ²¹That <u>I may cause those that love Me to inherit substance</u>; and <u>I will fill their treasures</u>.

◊

Hebrews 13:6 KJV
⁶So that <u>we may boldly say</u>, The LORD is my helper, and I will not fear what man shall do unto me.

◊

3 John 1:2 KJV
Beloved, <u>I wish</u> above all things <u>that thou mayest prosper</u> and be in health, even as thy soul prosper.

(*Be confident the heavenly Father God wants you to prosper in wealth <u>on earth</u>. Take heed to the underlined words.)

◊

✚

CHAPTER 2

<u>HOW TO MANAGE WEALTH WHILE IN ABUNDANT LIVING</u>

2

This chapter will provide you with scriptures on wisdom, knowledge and understanding to plan and to manage wealth through God's word. It will enlighten and instruct you on how to manage your daily life and financial affairs. Again, letting you witness from the Almighty that the abundant (money) life is for you. But avoid the love of money, meaning do not let it control you by causing you to do evil. God is love. By managing wealth through God's eyes, you will not fail because His instructions are perfect. I am a witness that He will reveal secret ways to managing wealth and you will always succeed. His word says, *"Every place that the sole of your foot tread upon, have I given that unto you!"* (Scripture reference *Joshua 1:3)*

2. HOW TO MANAGE WEALTH IN ABUNDANT LIVING

Deuteronomy 8:18 *KJV*

¹⁸But thou shalt <u>remember</u> the LORD thy God: <u>for it is He that giveth thee</u> power to get wealth<u>, that He may establish</u> His covenant which He sware unto thy fathers, as it is this day.

(*God is saying do not forget He endowed you with talent and the ability for wealth for <u>His purpose</u> (key word). Use and manage wealth wisely.)

◊

Proverbs 10:22 *KJV*

The blessing of the Lord <u>it</u> maketh rich, <u>and He</u> addeth no sorrow with it.
(*There was a time when I was believing God for the house I was renting. It came up for sale and I wanted to buy it. I had all the requirements to buy the house, but the owner sold it over the market price. I was so hurt, and I had 30 days to move.

A few years later after that incident God blessed me beyond my imagination with a home in a great community. One day that previous house situation came back to my memory, and I heard a voice say, the blessings from the Lord He make rich and add no sorrow to them. It was as if the Holy Spirit reminded me of that experience to illustrate this scripture. The other house was no comparison to my new house.)

◊

Proverbs 12:11 *KJV*
¹¹He that tilleth his land shall be satisfied with bread: but he that followeth vain persons is void of understanding.

◊

Ecclesiastes 2:26 *KJV*
For God giveth to a man that is good in his sight wisdom, and knowledge, and joy: but to the sinner he giveth travail, to gather and to heap up, that he may give to him that is good before God. This also is vanity and vexation of spirit.

◊

Luke 12:15 *KJV*

And He said unto them, "Take heed, and beware of covetousness, for a man's life consisteth not in the abundance of the things which he possesseth.

(* Everyone handles wealth differently. Riches or money reveal the true person, but sometimes even a well conscious person makes mistakes. This is why the scripture states to "be on the lookout as to how you perceive possessions". Manage your abundance properly.)

◊

Proverbs 22:4 *KJV*

By humility and the fear of the LORD are riches, and honour, and life.

◊

Psalms 1:1 *KJV*

Blessed is the man that walketh not in the counsel of the ungodly, nor standeth in the way of sinners, nor sitteth in the seat of the scornful...

(*I have always loved this verse. It manages every aspect of life! This

scripture has always energized my soul and is one of the reasons I can say I have a special relationship with the Lord.)

◊

Philippians 4:11-13 *KJV*
Not that I am speaking of being in need, for <u>I have learned in whatever situation</u> I am to be content. I <u>know how</u> to be <u>brought low</u>, and I know <u>how to abound.</u> In <u>any</u> and every <u>circumstance</u>, I have learned <u>the secret</u> of facing plenty and hunger, <u>abundance and need</u>. I can do all things through him who strengthens me.

(* Learn to become a master over your situations; everyone goes through tests and trials.)

◊

Proverbs 22:9 *KJV*
He that hath a <u>bountiful eye shall be blessed</u>; for he giveth of his bread to the poor.

◊

Luke 6:30 *KJV*

<u>Give to every man</u> that asketh of thee; and of him that taketh away thy goods ask them not again.

◊

1 Thessalonians 4:11-12 *KJV*

And that you study to be quietly, and <u>do your own business</u>, and to work with your hands, as we instructed you, so that you may walk <u>honestly toward them that are without</u>, and that ye may have lack of nothing.

◊

Luke 6:35 *KJV*

But love ye your enemies, and do good, and <u>lend</u>, <u>hoping for nothing again</u>; and your reward shall be great, and ye shall be the children of the Highest: for he is kind unto the unthankful and to the evil.

◊

Proverbs 19:4 *KJV*
<u>Wealth maketh many friends</u>; but the poor is separated from his neighbour.

> (*When living in abundance give to others and you will be blessed.)*

◊

Psalm 37:21 *KJV*
The wicked borroweth, and payeth not again: but the <u>righteous sheweth mercy, and giveth</u>.

◊

Galatians 6:7 *KJV*
Be not deceived; God is not mocked: for <u>whatsoever</u> a man <u>soweth</u>, that shall he also <u>reap</u>.

(Take mastership over managing your life wisely. whatever way you sow is what will manifest from the situation. Imagine this as like the power of the tongue, but flip it to the cause and effect of life situations. What you sow or do is what develops.)*

◊

Matthew 6:34 *KJV*

Take therefore no thought for the morrow: for the morrow shall take thought for the things of itself. Sufficient unto the day is the evil thereof.

(*Include declaring peace in your daily confession and meditation.)

✛
CHAPTER 3

GOD PREDESTINED PLANS FOR YOU WEALTHY

3

This chapter will enlighten you with scriptures to empower you with wisdom, knowledge and understanding of God's words revealing His plans for you in wealth, the Do's and Don'ts. It will grant you insight about strategic planning through God's eyes to influence your success. Whether you are implementing business principals, managing work, making investment decisions or everyday life situations your purpose in life is important to God. Keep in mind that you were predestined for a purpose on earth. You might have more than two gifts or talents. No matter what, once you have received revelation of your purpose put it into action and start the planning.

3. GOD PREDESTINED PLANS FOR YOU WEALTHY

Proverbs 21:5 KJV

The thoughts (*plans) of the diligent tend only to plenteousness; but of every one that is hasty only to want.

(* God will show you the end of what He endowed you to do on earth; then you must start the planning process knowing He will guide you. This is connected to your earthly wealth purpose. I learned from the bible the importance of planning. After you come into your known purpose on earth you must plan properly and thoroughly to bring it to life. There are many bible parables of planning. You must create a business plan to see a clear route in order to succeed in earthly business. Your wealthy place on earth was already predestined by God before you got here.)

◊

Psalm 40:5 *KJV*

Many, O LORD my God, are the wonderful works which thou hast done, and thy thoughts (*plans) which are to us-ward: they cannot be reckoned up in order unto Thee: <u>if I would declare and speak of them,</u> they are more than could be numbered.

(* Seek out God's purpose for your life then start planning.)

◊

Luke 14:28-30 *KJV*

For which of you, <u>intending to build a tower, sitteth not down first, and counteth the cost, whether he have sufficient to finish it</u>. [29]Lest haply, after he hath laid the foundation, and is not able to finish it, all that behold it begin to mock him, [30]Saying, This man began to build, and was not able to finish.

(* This is a perfect example of the importance of setting up the planning which will allows you to see the future.)

◊

Proverbs 24:3-4 KJV
<u>Through wisdom</u> is an house builded; and <u>by understanding</u> it is established: ₄ And <u>by knowledge</u> shall the chambers be filled with all precious and pleasant riches.

◊

Proverbs 28:19 KJV
<u>He that tilleth</u> his land <u>shall have plenty</u> of bread: but he that followeth after vain persons shall have poverty enough.

(* Plan properly and you will end well.)

◊

Proverbs 13:11 KJV
Wealth gotten by vanity ₁ shall be diminished: but he that gathereth by labour shall increase.

(* Orderly plan obtaining wealth, step by step and you win.)

◊

Proverbs 10:4 KJV
He becometh poor that dealeth with a slack hand: but the hand of *the diligent* maketh rich.

◊

Proverbs 20:4 KJV
The sluggard will not plow by reason of the cold; therefore shall he beg in harvest, and have nothing.

◊

Hebrews 13:5 KJV
Let your conversation be without covetousness; and be content with such things as ye have: for he hath said, I will never leave thee, nor forsake thee.

◊

Luke 16:9 KJV
And I say unto you, make to yourselves friends of the mammon of unrighteousness; that, when ye fail [*don't have], they may receive you everlasting habitations.

◊

1 Timothy 5:8 *KJV*

But <u>if any provide not for his own</u>, and specially for those of his own <u>house</u>, he hath denied the faith, and is worse than an infidel.

◊

1 Timothy 6:17-19 *KJV*

Charge them that are rich in this world, that they be not highminded, nor trust in uncertain riches, but in the living God, who giveth us richly all things to enjoy; ₁₈ That they do good, that they be rich in good works, ready to distribute, willing to communicate; ₁₉ <u>Laying up in store for themselves a good foundation against the time to come</u>, that they may lay hold on eternal life.

◊

Proverbs 6:6-8 *KJV*

Go to the ant, thou sluggard; <u>consider her ways, and be wise</u>: ₇ Which having no guide, overseer, or ruler, ₈ Provideth her meat in the summer, and gathereth her food in the harvest.

◊

37

Philippians 4:6 *KJV*
<u>Be careful for nothing</u>; but in every thing by prayer and supplication with thanksgiving let your requests be made known unto God.

◊

Romans 13:8 *KJV*
Owe no man any thing, but to love one another: for he that loveth another hath fulfilled the law.

◊

Acts 20:35 *KJV*
I have shewed you all things, how that so labouring ye ought to support the weak, and to remember the words of the Lord Jesus, how he said, It is more blessed to give than to receive.

◊

Matthew 25:14-28 *KJV*
14 ...As a man travelling into a far country, who called his own servants, 15 And unto one he gave five talents, to another two, and to another one; to every man according to his several ability; 20 And so he that had

received five talents came and brought other five talents, saying, Lord, I have gained beside them five talents more. ₂₁ His lord said unto him, Well done, ...enter thou into the joy of thy lord. ₂₂ He also that had received two gained two...His lord said unto him, Well done, enter thou into the joy of thy lord. ₂₄ Then he which had received the one talent came and said, Lord, ₂₅ I was afraid, and went and hid thy talent in the earth: ₂₆ His lord answered and said unto him, Thou wicked and slothful servant ₂₈ Take therefore the talent from him, and give it unto him which hath ten talents.

(* Your talents and gifts within you are powers to your wealth on earth.)

◊

Matthew 5:42 *KJV*
<u>Give</u> to him that asketh thee,
and from him that would borrow
of thee turn not thou away.

◊

Proverbs 28:27 KJV
He that giveth unto the poor shall not lack: but he that hideth his eyes shall have many a curse.

◊

Proverbs 28:20 KJV
A faithful man shall abound with blessings: but he that maketh haste to be rich shall not be innocent.

◊

Isaiah 60:11 KJV
Therefore your gates shall be open continually; they shall not be shut day nor night; that men may bring unto thee the forces of the Gentiles, and that their kings may be brought.

◊

Proverbs 27:23 KJV
<u>Be thou diligent to know</u> the state of thy flocks, and look well to thy herds.

◊

Colossians 3:23 KJV
And whatsoever ye do, do it heartily, as to the Lord, and not unto men;

◊

Exodus 23:12 KJV
Six days thou shalt do thy work, and on the seventh day thou shalt rest: that thine ox and thine ass may rest, and the son of thy handmaid, and the stranger, may be refreshed.

(*Be kind to those who labor with you in business and others.)

✢

CHAPTER 4

<u>INVEST YOUR WEALTH</u>

4

This chapter is about investing very wisely and strategically while you are in abundance (with plenty money). Each scripture below provides examples about investments. The Lord has purposed you to win in prosperity. The scriptures are wisdom from God's words. The greatest investment is to seek first the Kingdom of God and His righteousness and everything else will be added to you.

4. <u>INVEST YOUR WEALTH</u>

(Take heed to the underlined words,
they are profound for investing.)*

Proverbs 31:18 KJV
She <u>perceiveth</u> that her merchandise is
<u>good</u>: her candle goeth not out by night.

◊

Luke 6:38 KJV
<u>Give</u>, and <u>it shall be given unto you</u>;
good <u>measure</u>, pressed down, and
shaken together, and running over, shall
men give into your bosom. For with
the same measure that ye mete withal
<u>it shall be measured to you again</u>.

*(*Give in the areas of friendship, money,
loving mankind, praying for other's
wellbeing and goodness for their lives,
smiling, saying encouraging words to
others, spreading joy, implementing
peace and give tithes and offering.)*

◊

Matthew 25:27-29 *KJV*

Thou oughtest therefore to have <u>put</u> (*invest)<u> my money to the exchangers</u>, and then at my coming I should have received mine own with usury. ₂₈ <u>Take therefore the talent from him, and give it unto him which hath ten talents</u>. ₂₉ For unto every one that hath shall be given, and <u>he shall have abundance</u>: but from him that hath not shall be taken away even that which he hath.

(*Know your purpose on this earth. Do not ignore your God given talent within, use it. If you don't use your talent, you will lack.*)

◊

Proverbs 3:9-10 *KJV*

<u>Honour the LORD with thy substance</u> (*wealth), and with the firstfruits of all thine increase: ₁₀ So shall thy barns <u>be filled with plenty</u>, and thy presses shall burst out with new wine.

(* *Understand the Lord endowed you a purpose to gain wealth on earth as his assistant, so He may establish His plans* *through you. He will ensure you obtain a return.)*

◊

Malachi 3:10 KJV
Bring ye all the tithes into the storehouse, that there may be meat in mine house, and prove me now herewith, saith the LORD of hosts, if I will not open you the windows of heaven, and pour you out a blessing, that there shall not be room enough to receive it.

◊

Ecclesiastes 11:1-2 KJV
<u>Cast thy bread</u> upon the waters: for <u>thou shalt find it after many days</u>. ₂ Give <u>a portion </u>to seven, and also to eight; for thou knowest not what evil shall be upon the earth.

◊

Proverbs 31:16 KJV
She considereth a field, and buyeth it: with the fruit of her hands she planteth a vineyard.

◊

Matthew 6:20-21 *KJV*

But lay up for yourselves treasures in heaven where neither moth nor rust corrupt, and where thieves do not break in and steal. $_{21}$ For where your treasure is, there will your heart be also.

(* Lay up for yourselves treasures in heaven in addition to managing earthly affairs.)

◊

Proverbs 31:24 *KJV*

She maketh fine linen, and selleth it; and delivereth girdles unto the merchant.

◊

Luke 12:33-34 *KJV*

Sell that ye have, and give alms; provide yourselves bags which wax not old, a treasure in the heavens that faileth not, where no thief approacheth, neither moth corrupteth. $_{34}$ For where your treasure is, there will your heart be also.

◊

1 Corinthians 16:2 KJV

Upon the first day of the week let every one of you <u>lay by him in store</u>, as God hath prospered him, that there be no gatherings when I come.

(* Save and invest, putting money aside for surplus needs.)

◊

Proverbs 28:8 KJV

<u>He that</u> by usury and unjust gain <u>increaseth his substance</u> (*wealth), he shall gather it for him that will pity the poor.

◊

＋

CHAPTER 5

STAY MINDFUL OF LIVING IN THE SECRET PLACE OF THE MOST-HIGH ONCE YOU ARE IN ABUNDANCE

5

This chapter will reveal and equip you with scriptures and knowledge from God's words to stay self-conscious in abundant living, practice wisdom, be mindful of how to deal with others, and treat humanity with Godly love. Stay vigilant, understanding that the love of money is the root to all kinds of evil. A wise man hears the Father's instructions and performs them.

To stay mindful of living in the secret place of the most-high once you are in abundant living is to keep your eyes and heart on the creator of your purpose. Set aside time for prayer, meditation and praying in the Spirit. These days it is imperative to continue in prayer without ceasing. Do you know why God says pray without ceasing? It is because God knows the world is and will always be saturated with worldly interruptions and events designed to keep us distracted.

In addition to the scriptures in this chapter which provide you knowledge and insight; the fundamental way to *pray without ceasing* is to remain in the secret place of the most High by *"praying in the Spirit"*. This is the answer! God will endow you with so much insight. How do you do this? Number one, ensure you have a relationship with the Father; two, the Holy Spirit dwelling within you and three, practice praying at all times.

Again, a wise man hears the Father's instructions and performs them.

5. STAY MINDFUL OF LIVING IN THE SECRET PLACE OF THE MOST-HIGH ONCE YOU ARE IN ABUNDANCE

Jeremiah 29:11 *KJV*
For I know the thoughts that I think toward you, saith the LORD, thoughts of peace, and not of evil, to give you an expected end.

◊

1 Timothy 6:6 *KJV*
But godliness with contentment
is great gain.

◊

1 Kings 9:4-5 *KJV*
And <u>if thou wilt walk before me</u>, as David thy father walked, in integrity of heart, and in uprightness, <u>to do according to all that I have commanded thee</u>, and wilt keep my statutes and my judgments: ⁵Then I will establish the throne of thy kingdom upon Israel forever, <u>as I promised</u> to David thy father, saying, <u>There shall not fail thee</u> a man upon the throne of Israel.

Psalm 62:10 *KJV*

Trust not in oppression, and become 1
not vain in robbery: if riches increase,
set not your heart upon them.

Matthew 13:22 *KJV*

He also that received seed among the
thorns is he that heareth the word; and the
care of this world, and the deceitfulness of
riches, choke the word, and he becometh
unfruitful.

◊

1 Timothy 5:8 *KJV*

But if any provide not for his own, and
specially for those of his own house, he
hath denied the faith, and is worse than
an infidel.

◊

Matthew 6:24 *KJV*

No man can serve two masters: for
either he will hate the one, and love
the other; or else he will hold to the
one, and despise the other. Ye cannot
serve God and mammon (*money).

◊

Proverbs 11:4 KJV

Riches profit not in the day of wrath: but righteousness delivereth from death.

◊

Ecclesiastes 5:10 KJV

He that loveth silver (*money) shall not be satisfied with silver; nor he that loveth abundance with increase: this is also vanity.

◊

Proverbs 11:28 KJV

He that <u>trusteth in his riches shall fall</u>: but the righteous shall flourish as ad a branch.

◊

Proverbs 12:2 KJV

A good man <u>obtaineth favour of the LORD</u>: but a man of wicked devices b will he condemn.

◊

Proverbs 13:1-20 KJV

<u>A wise</u> son (*person) <u>heareth</u> his father's <u>instruction</u>: but a scorner a <u>heareth not</u> rebuke. ₂ A man shall eat good by

the fruit of his mouth. ₆ Righteousness keepeth him that is upright in the way: but wickedness overthroweth the sinner. ₇ There is that maketh himself rich, yet hath nothing: ₁₀ Only by pride cometh contention: ₁₁ Wealth gotten by vanity shall be diminished: but he that gathereth by labour shall increase. ₁₄ The law of the wise is a fountain of life... ₁₅ Good understanding giveth favour: ₂₀ He that walketh with wise men shall be wise: but a companion of fools shall be destroyed.

◊

Proverbs 22:16 *KJV*
He that oppresseth the poor to increase his riches, and he that giveth to the rich, shall surely come to want.

◊

1 Timothy 6:10 *KJV*
For the love of money is the root of all evil: which while some covetd after, they have erred from the faith, and pierced themselves through with many sorrows.

◊

Luke 16:11 *KJV*

If therefore <u>ye have not been faithful</u> in the unrighteous mammon, who will commit to your trust the true riches.

◊

1 Timothy 6:6-9 *KJV*

But <u>godliness with contentment is great gain</u>. ₇ For we brought nothing into this world, and it is certain we can carry nothing out. ₈ And having food and raimen let us be therewith content. ₉ <u>But</u> they that will be rich fall into temptation and a snare, and into many foolish and hurtful lusts, which drown men in destruction and perdition.

Job 27:16-17 *KJV*

Though he heap up silver as the dust, and prepare raiment as the clay; ¹⁷ He may prepare it, but the just shall put it on, and <u>the innocent shall divide the silver</u>.

◊

James 2:15-16 *KJV*

[15]If a brother or sister be naked, and <u>destitute of daily food</u>, [16]And one of you say unto them, Depart in peace, be ye warmed and filled; notwithstanding ye give them not those things which are needful to the body; what doth it profit?

(*Give to humanity without turning them way lacking.)

◊

Luke 16:13 *NKJV*

<u>No servant can serve two masters:</u> for either he will hate the one, and love the other; or else he will hold to the one, and despise the other. <u>You cannot serve God and mammon</u>.

◊

Luke 15:13 *KJV*

[13] And <u>not many days after</u> the younger son gathered all together, and took his journey into a far country, and there wasted his substance with riotous living.

◊

Proverbs 23:4-5 *KJV*

Labour not to be rich: <u>cease from thine own wisdom</u>. ⁵Wilt thou set thine eyes upon that which is not? for riches certainly make themselves wings; they fly away as an eagle toward heaven.

CHAPTER 6

FAITH IS THE KEY

6

This chapter sums it all up! God has declared that without faith it is impossible to please Him. This chapter is about one of the ultimate keys that will place you on the front row with the Heavenly Father! To receive the answer regarding your purpose in life, your faith is required. To get prayers answered, your faith is required. To call upon God and believe that He hears you, will deliver you, and help you in times of trouble; your faith is required. To understand His angels, hearken unto the voice of His word to help you in time of need, your faith is required. To believe before you were born God endowed you with purpose and talents that will transition you into wealth, your faith is required. "Now Faith Is" said the Lord of Almighty.

6. <u>FAITH IS THE KEY</u>

Hebrews 11:1-6 <small>KJV</small>

<u>**Now**</u> **faith is** the substance of **things** hoped for, the **evidence** of things not seen.

² For **by it** the elders obtained a good report.

³ **Through faith** we understand that the worlds were framed by the word of God, so that things which are seen were not made of things which do appear. (*made by man.*)

⁴ **By faith** Abel offered unto God a more excellent sacrifice than Cain, by which he obtained witness that he was righteous, God testifying of his gifts:

⁵ **By faith** Enoch was translated that he should not see death; and was not found, because God had translated him: for before his translation he had this testimony, that he pleased God.

⁶ **But without faith** *it is* **impossible to please** *Him*: for he that cometh to God

must believe that He is, and that He is a rewarder of them that diligently seek him.

◊

Psalms 24:1 *KJV*

The earth *is* the LORD'S, and the fulness thereof; the world, and they that dwell therein!

✚

CHAPTER 7

<u>GET ANSWERS FROM GOD IN THE SECRET PLACE</u>

7

This chapter provide mysteries about entering and communicating in the secret place of the Almighty. Matthew will give you clues on activating the heavenly dimension through the Supreme Direction. Psalms 91 is also one of God's secret places. The bible is saturated with Gods secrets, but you have to be attuned with the Holy Spirit to recognize them. If you meditate on these verses in this chapter and pray in the Holy Spirit which is the key here; then you will be enlightened, encouraged, empowered, and receive great wisdom. Matthew shows you how to call unto Him and He will show you great and mighty things you cannot see with the natural eye. "Trust in the Lord with all of your heart and lean not unto your own understanding" Proverbs 3:5.

7. GET ANSWERS FROM GOD IN THE SECRET PLACE

Psalms 91:1 KJV
He that *dwelleth in* the secret place of the most High shall abide under the shadow of the Almighty.

(*The **secret place** is having a personal relationship with the Lord; spending time in prayer by praying in the Holy Spirit without ceasing, then *listening* for the answers.)

◊

Jeremiah 33:3 KJV
Call to me, and I will answer you, and *show you great and mighty things*, which you know not.

(* One of those great and mighty things is your purpose in life.)

◊

Jeremiah 1:5 *KJV*

Before <u>I formed</u> you in the belly <u>I knew thee</u> <u>(*you)</u>;

(* *God Almighty is the Beginning and the End, the ULTIMATE POWER.*)

The Supreme Direction

Mathew 6:9-13 _KJV_

⁹ After this manner _therefore pray ye_: _Our Father which art in heaven_, Hallowed be thy name.

◊

₁₀ Thy kingdom <u>come</u>. Thy will be done <u>in</u> <u>earth</u>, as _it is_ <u>in</u> heaven.
(* As you have already designed me in heaven, transform me into my purpose on earth.)

◊

₁₁ _Give us <u>this</u> <u>day</u> our <u>daily bread</u>._
(* By your mercies that are new everyday, God feed me Your bread which is Your Word. Also order my steps in your word.)

◊

12 And *forgive us* our debts, as we forgive our debtors.

(* Help me see clear how critical forgiveness is so I will not hold up my blessings, and stay physically healthy.)

◊

13 And *lead us not into temptation* but deliver us *from evil*: For thine is the kingdom, and the power, and the glory, forever. Amen.

(* Order my steps, keep me from evil.)

ABOUT THE AUTHOR

The author, Bernita Burries-Mason was born and raised in Southern California (CA). She grew up in the Los Angeles county area. Bernita is the founder of Opulent Global Products Inc., in Anaheim, CA. where she enjoys doing business and managing the daily operations of the company. Bernita is certified by the Women Business Enterprise National Council-West location as a Women Business Enterprise (WBE). She holds a Bachelor of Arts Degree in Sociology and in Business Administration along with other credentials. Bernita amassed more than 26 years of experience in administration, quality assurance, management, leadership, project management, strategic planning, customer relations and more while working 25 years with one of the world's largest leading aircraft company in Long Beach, CA.

She enjoys bowling, singing, traveling, going on weekend outings, walking, exercising is a must, hiking, being health conscious, attending church, loving people and more. Golfing is on her list to learn.

Bernita was inspired to write this book, because she wanted to understand God's wisdom about money and prosperity. She began to search the bible about money and all she could say was "wow". The bible unveiled how to manage money, give money to humanity, master control of money but not allow it to take control, most of all how to use money to support the kingdom of Heaven and a host of things. This was her true breakthrough. She was amazed at how much the Lord cared. Immediately after getting this understanding, the Lord said now put this in a book for others who want to understand My wisdom about money on earth. Money is the answer to all things. **Do not** pervert it with _the Love_ of money which is the root of all evil.

("_The earth is the LORD'S, and the fulness thereof; the world, and they that dwell therein_") _Psalms 24:1._

<u>Acknowledgements</u>

*I give the highest thanks to the most High,
the forever lifter of my soul, He is my
genuine friend Jesus Christ hello Lord ☺
You are awesome. Thank you for inspiring
and empowering me to write this book.*

◊

*I am incredibly grateful and would
like to truly thank Gwendolyn Burries
for her help with this book.*

◊

*I want to thank you AuthorHouse
Publishing, for publishing this book.*

◊

*My son Everett, I am proud of
you. I am pleased to witness you*

*staying focused and transitioning
into success at a young age.
You inspire me.*

◊

*To my late mother, Ibera, for
being an awesome lady in my
life, you rocked, thanks mom.*

The Comforter Is Waiting
Let Him Help You

The Comforter is waiting to help you walk through all of life situations and circumstances on earth, to bring the manifestation of your God given wealthy purpose into existence. Who is the comforter? He is the Holy Spirit, the third power of the trinity "Father, Son and Holy Spirit". The power of God. Your earthly personal assistant from heaven, isn't this awesome! Jesus love you so much this is what He said *But the Helper, the Holy Spirit, whom the Father will send in my name, he will teach you all things and bring to your remembrance all that I have said to you. John 14:26*

I am a living witness; the Comforter will assist with living out your known purpose!

NOTES

_____

_____

_____

_____

_____

_____

_____

_____

_____

_____

_____

_____

_____

_____

_____

_____

NOTES

--- --- --- --- --- --- --- --- --- --- --- --- --- --- --- --- --- --- ---

NOTES

NOTES

_____

_____

_____

_____

_____

_____

_____

_____

_____

_____

_____

_____

_____

_____

_____

_____

_____

_____

NOTES

NOTES

NOTES

NOTES

NOTES

_____

_____

_____

_____

_____

_____

_____

_____

_____

_____

_____

_____

_____

_____

_____

_____

_____

_____

NOTES

_____

_____

_____

_____

_____

_____

_____

_____

_____

_____

_____

_____

_____

_____

_____

_____

_____

NOTES

＋

_____

_____

_____

_____

_____

_____

_____

_____

_____

_____

_____

_____

_____

_____

_____

_____

_____

_____

_____

Printed in the United States
By Bookmasters